CLEVELAND STEAMER

AND HIS FAITHFUL DOG

BLUMPKIN

by **Jolly Zak**

Editor's Note

My great-uncle Arshcloch Scheisse befriended Jolly Zak during World War I, when they both landed in a military hospital after consuming too much Liberty Sausage. My great-uncle was sent home on a medical discharge, and Jolly Zak followed close behind, a refugee from the war torn Vulgaria.

Jolly Zak lived in my great-uncle's shed until the day he died. I don't know what he did, although I'm pretty sure I was named after him. I remember that his shed was very dark, and smelled like Colgate and hair.

I found this book in the shed's sub-basement, while I was getting ready to burn it down. It looks like a children's book, and it seems like it's very sweet and has a nice little ecological message. But I think some of these things have different meanings than they used to. But it also seems like a nice little story. It's all very confusing. Enjoy!

For Koss and Leslie. Sorry.
For the BVs. Inspirational.

All rights reserved. This book or any portion thereof may not be reproduced or used in any manner whatsoever without the express written permission of the publisher except for the use of brief quotations in a book review.

Copyright © 2016 by Zak Klobucher
First Printing, 2016

ISBN 978-0-9975716-0-8

A Crack Publisher
4027 Invierno Drive, Unit B
Santa Barbara, CA 93110

www.JollyZak.com

Cleveland was a regular ship
A steamer strong and true
He rode upon the Mississip'
a river wide and blue

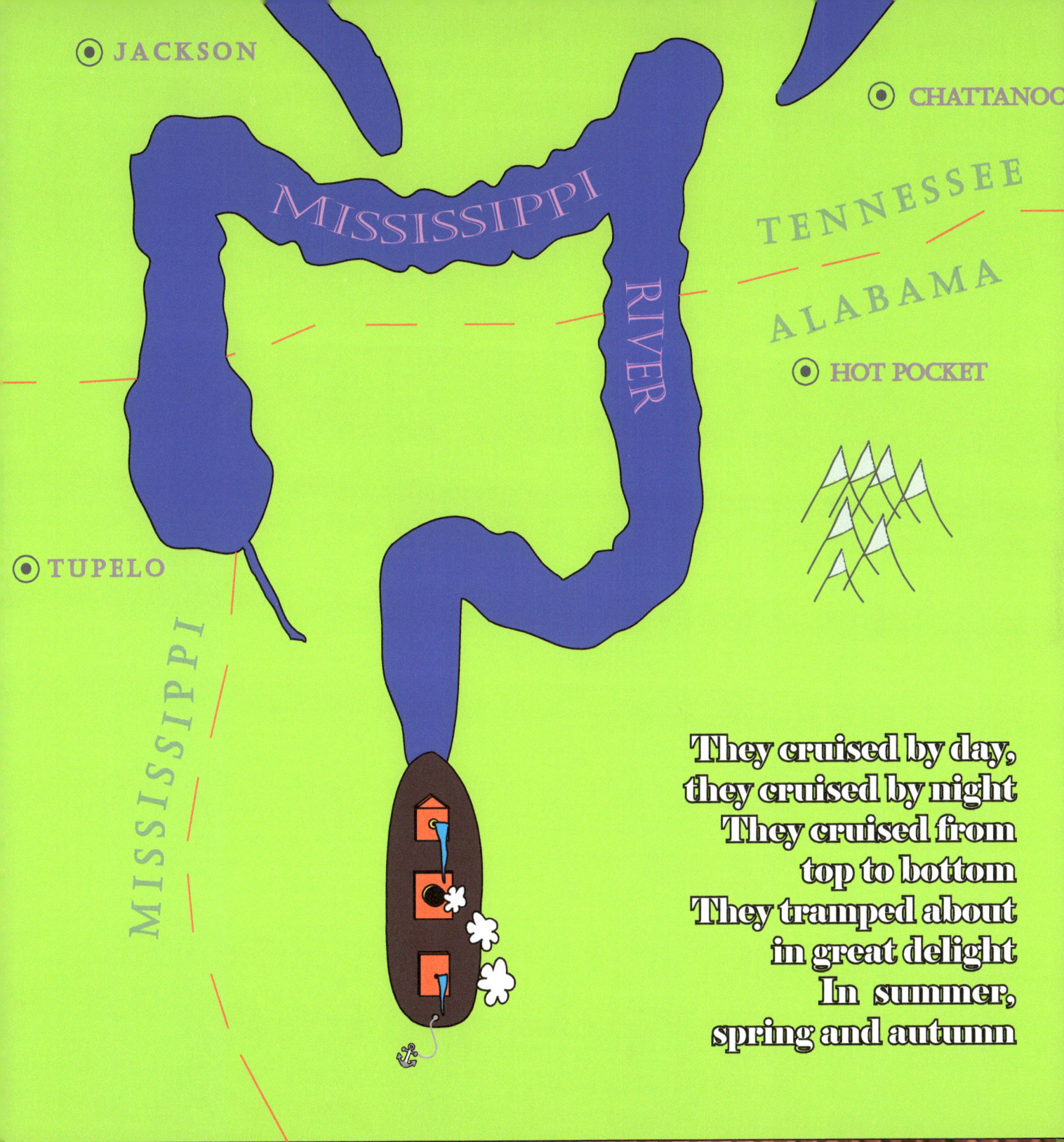

They raced upstream to find the source
Of what befouled the river
They found a wall that blocked the course
A smell that made them shiver

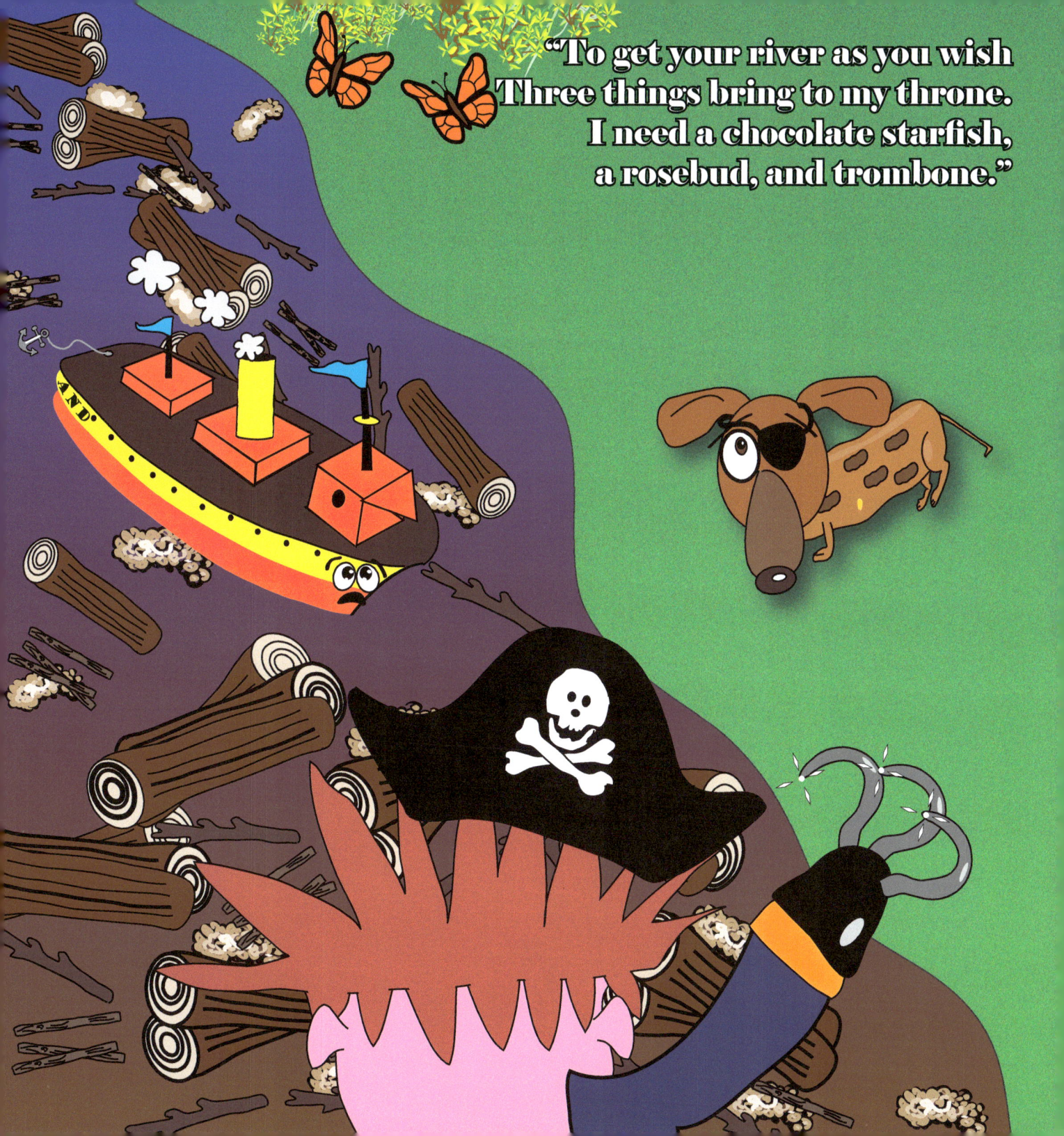

They tried to hide behind a tree
Disguised to look like elves
But none would make the river free
Only they could save themselves

They searched by day, they searched by night
To do this solemn duty
They searched beneath the full moon light
To find the Pirate's booty

**The final prize still to be found
They almost took a pass
They didn't know that trombone sound
Had to learn this piece of brass**

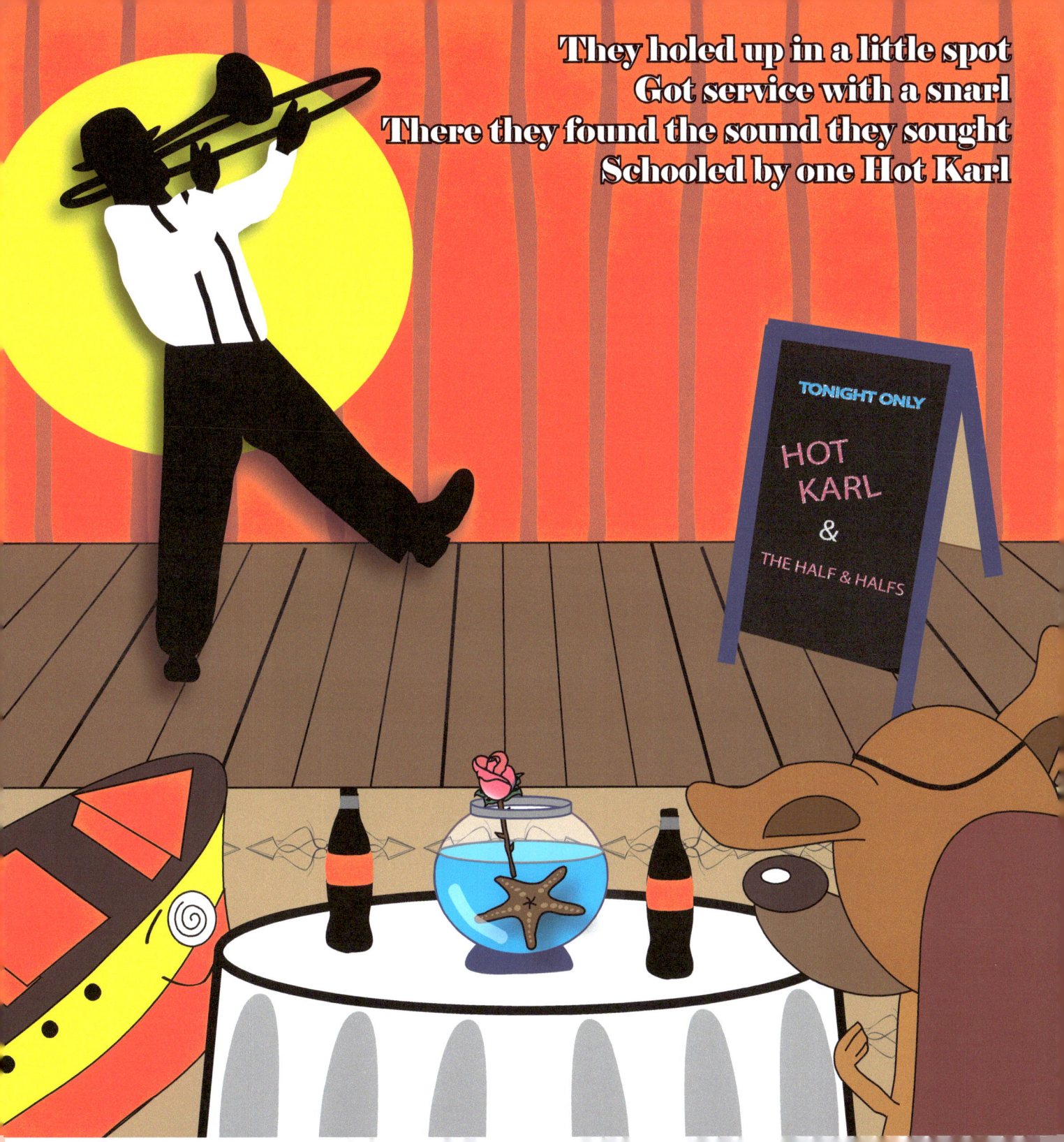

But Karl's 'bone was not the one
To give them the big save
So they trudged on 'til they were done
And finally found a cave

Three things they brought to Felch's throne
But was he thrilled to see them?
He sniffed the rose and blew the 'bone
The starfish, he did eat him

They'd been tricked, their quest for naught
Felch he squelched his pledge
Would this be the money shot
To push them off the edge?

No! They were heroes and not dogs
Felch he had not awed 'em
They slammed the dam and pinched off logs
Hard wood they quickly sawed 'em

With all their friends they tore it down
The best that they could do
The river free! They beat that clown!
Then Felch yelled out...

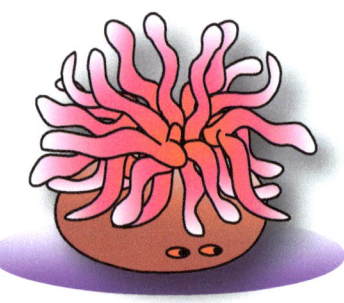

So toss a salad and pack some fudge
For a victory lunch
They had great fun, so we won't judge
This happy, carefree bunch

END

About the Author

Jolly Zak fled Vulgaria at the height of World War I, seeking a better life. He arrived on the shores of the United States with nothing but half a pocket and a tattered copy of Adobe Illustrator. He's dead now.